by MARGARET MORAN

Table of Contents

Chapter 1 The Louisiana Purchase 2

Chapter 2 Preparing for the Expedition 6

Chapter 3 From St. Louis to Fort Mandan 10

Chapter 4 Winter at Fort Mandan 14

Chapter 5 From Fort Mandan to the Pacific Ocean . . .18

Chapter 6 The Return Trip 26

Glossary 31

Index 32

The Louisiana Purchase

In 1776, the new United States was much smaller than it is today. It reached from the northern tip of Maine to the southern border of Georgia. The western boundary was the Mississippi River. The nation remained that size until 1803. In that year, France agreed to sell the United States a vast area of land west of the Mississippi River. This area was called the Louisiana Territory.

Originally, President Thomas Jefferson had offered to buy only the port city of New Orleans from France. For those Americans living on the western edge of the frontier, a port from which to ship their goods to Europe was needed. But because the French government needed money, it offered to sell all of the Louisiana Territory.

▲ Thomas Jefferson was the third president of the United States. He served from 1801 to 1809.

At first, President Jefferson worried that the Constitution didn't give the national government the power to buy territory. But Jefferson's advisers, including James Madison, a lawyer and future president, persuaded him that it did. So for the sum of $15 million (a little more than $237 million in today's dollars), the United States bought 830,000 square miles (about 2,150,000 square kilometers) of land.

This purchase was called the Louisiana Purchase. It doubled the size of the United States. It was also a real bargain! The price broke down to about $286 a square mile, or about 45 cents an acre in today's dollars.

▼ The Louisiana Purchase doubled the land area of the United States.

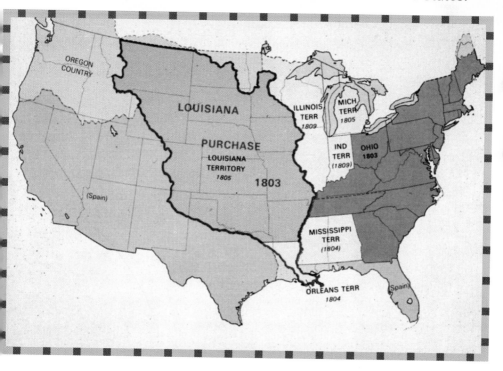

Jefferson had been interested in the Louisiana Territory even before the United States bought the area. He knew about the early European explorers' idea of a **Northwest Passage**—an all-water route to the Pacific Ocean. Jefferson had his secretary, Meriwether Lewis, plan a secret **expedition** into the Louisiana Territory. Once the French sold the Louisiana Territory to the United States, the expedition no longer had to be a secret.

Now that the United States owned Louisiana, Jefferson could learn more about the area: How livable was it? Could people make a living and raise families there? Did a water route to the Pacific run through it? Lewis now had the job of leading the expedition to find out.

IT'S A FACT!

Meriwether Lewis was born in Virginia and spent time along the frontier as a soldier. A friend of President Jefferson, he became his secretary in 1801. Following the expedition, Lewis was named governor of the Louisiana Territory.

William Clark was older than Lewis and more experienced as a frontiersman. After the expedition, Clark was made superintendent of Native American affairs for the government. In 1813, he became governor of the Missouri Territory, which had been part of the Louisiana Purchase.

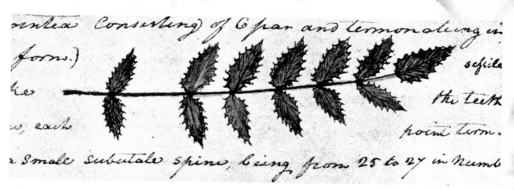

▲ Lewis made this drawing of an evergreen shrub leaf in his journal.

Lewis asked his friend William Clark to join the expedition as co-captain. Jefferson named the group the Corps of Discovery and instructed them to:

- see if they could find a safe, easy, all-water route to the Pacific Ocean
- make friends with the Native Americans of the area
- make careful observations of the plants, animals, minerals, climate, and land features.

Lewis and Clark were to send **specimens** of the animals, plants, and minerals they found to Washington, D.C., for examination.

IT'S A FACT!

Lewis and Clark kept **journals** of the trip. The journals explained what the Corps of Discovery found in this new territory. Lewis and Clark made maps of the land they traveled across, noting rivers, waterfalls, and mountains. They drew pictures of plants, flowers, trees, birds, and other animals—whatever they saw. The men of the Lewis and Clark expedition were the first non-Native Americans to see many of these things and travel much of this land.

Preparing for the Expedition

(December 1803 to April 1804)

During the winter of 1803–1804, Lewis and Clark made preparations for their expedition. They had to recruit men for the Corps of Discovery, buy supplies, and have boats built. The two leaders chose 27 men to journey to the Pacific Ocean and back. Four other men were to go along on the first part of the trip only. They would return after the first winter, taking with them the first specimens of animals, plants, and minerals for Jefferson. Along the way, the Corps would also hire guides and interpreters.

The men of the Corps were between the ages of 20 and 35. Only two were married. Some of the men had been soldiers, blacksmiths, and gunsmiths. One had been a carpenter.

IT'S A FACT!

William Clark was the chief cartographer, or mapmaker, for the expedition. In all, he drew 60 maps. Some maps spread across several sheets of paper and were eight feet long and four feet wide. Clark used the compass shown here to navigate and to compile the distances he would use for his maps.

Among the 27 men on the expedition was York, an African American slave. Slavery still existed in the United States in 1803. York was a big man, and his size and color fascinated the Native Americans that he met on the trail. York proved a good scout and trader.

The Corps set up their camp near St. Louis, Missouri, on the Mississippi River. They spent the winter of 1803–1804 there. Lewis bought supplies in Philadelphia and had them shipped to the camp. Those supplies included:

- flannel shirts, woolen pants, coats, shoes, and socks for each member of the Corps
- 150 yards of cloth to be made into tents
- blankets and **knapsacks**
- lead and gunpowder to be made into bullets
- knives, fish hooks, and fishing line
- tools such as saws, chisels, and pliers.

☑ Point

WRITE ABOUT IT

Why do you think the men needed those supplies? Write down your answer and share it with a group member.

The Corps wanted to find an all-water route to the Pacific Ocean. Lewis and Clark hoped that they would be able to sail from the Mississippi River to the Pacific Ocean. To do this, they would need to have boats.

Lewis himself designed the **keelboat**, the largest of the watercraft. The keelboat had a cabin, storage lockers, and places for 20 oars. The boat could be **poled** as well as rowed. At times, the men even pulled the boat along. They tied ropes to it, waded into the river near the riverbanks, and pulled the boat after them up the river. The keelboat carried most of the supplies.

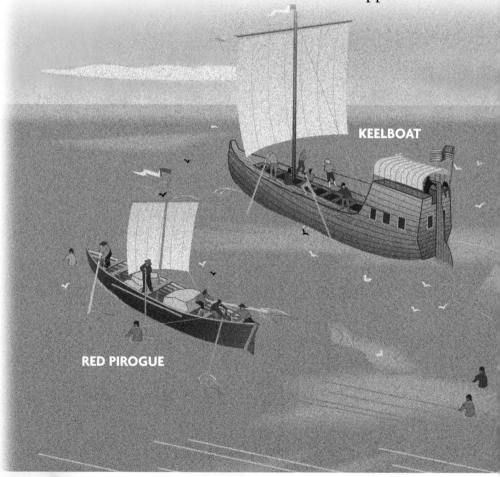

KEELBOAT

RED PIROGUE

The Corps had two large canoes called **pirogues** (PEH-rohgz), which also carried supplies. Both pirogues had sails and used crews of up to eight men. At times, the pirogues too, had to be poled and pulled **upstream**, against the flow of the river.

Along the way, the rivers became too dangerous for the larger boats. The men then had to carve **dugout canoes** out of tree trunks. The canoes held four to six men. In their three-year journey to the Pacific and back, the Corps built 15 canoes.

DUGOUT CANOE

WHITE PIROGUE

IT'S A FACT!

The Corps of Discovery expected to hunt and fish for their food. But in case they couldn't find enough to eat, Clark had bought 193 pounds of "portable soup." This was a thick paste of beef, eggs, and vegetables. The paste was made by boiling the ingredients until all the liquid had disappeared. On the trail, the men just had to add water and heat. It was the first instant soup!

From St. Louis to Fort Mandan

(May to November 1804)

On May 14, 1804, the Corps of Discovery set off from their camp near St. Louis. They sailed up the Mississippi and into the Missouri River. Two months later, they were still on the Missouri. Their top speed was 14 miles a day. Often it was much less—perhaps five miles a day.

They traveled this slowly because they were traveling upstream, which was against the current. Usually, the men could move forward only if they rowed or poled the heavy keelboat. The boat's sail wasn't very useful against the strong current.

The river held dangers such as floating logs that could ram a boat and **sandbars** that could cause it to get stuck. In their early days on the Missouri, Clark wrote of the trouble the men had in getting the keelboat off a sandbar.

It's a Fact!

An unusual member of the Corps was Lewis's dog, Seaman. He was a Newfoundland, a breed shown in the photo at the left. Various journal entries note Seaman's value to the Corps. He chased after game for them and kept watch at night, warning the men of approaching dangers such as grizzly bears.

As the men continued upstream, the country changed dramatically. They left wooded areas behind and floated through a vast, treeless grassland. The Corps of Discovery had come to the **Great Plains**. They were among the first non-Native Americans to see the plains and the huge herds of buffalo.

The Missouri River begins in the mountains and flows through the Great Plains. The Corps would not reach the mountains until the fall of 1804. ▼

MAKE CONNECTIONS

The daily schedule of the Corps of Discovery looked like this.

- Up with the Sun and have breakfast
- Break camp and begin travel on the river by 7
- Stop for dinner and rest at midday
- Travel on the river until early evening
- Make camp and eat
- Prepare for the next day
- Bed down or keep watch

How does this compare with your daily schedule?

▲ The figure of Thomas Jefferson is on one side of the
Peace Medal and a handshake is on the other side.

One of the tasks Jefferson had given Lewis and Clark was to make friends with the Native American peoples they met. There were few Native Americans along the first part of the Missouri River. It was not until August that the Corps met a group of Missouri and Oto Native Americans, and later a **band** of Yankton Sioux.

At each encounter, Lewis and Clark invited the chiefs to a council. The members of the Corps dressed in their military uniforms and paraded past the Native Americans. Lewis and Clark showed the chiefs the "magic" of magnets and **compasses**, and let them look through the small telescopes that the Corps used.

The captains also gave the chiefs Jefferson Peace Medals. These medals had been made specially for this purpose by order of the president. The captains also gave the chiefs other presents that Lewis had bought in Philadelphia.

All went well with these meetings until the Corps came to the territory of the Teton Sioux. The Teton, also known as the Lakota, were the most powerful Native American nation in the region. They controlled all trade and did not want to lose this control to American traders.

The Teton chiefs threatened the Corps and told them to turn back. Both sides showed off their weapons. Twice, the Corps and the Teton warriors almost came to blows. But after four days of meetings, the Teton let the Corps continue north.

IT'S A FACT!

The Corps carried hundreds of pounds of what Lewis called in his journal "Indian Presents." He spent $669.50 (more than $10,000 in today's dollars) for such things as:

- 33 pounds of colored beads
- 4,600 sewing needles
- many yards of cloth
- 30 cotton shirts
- 288 knives
- 4 bottles of perfume
- combs made of ivory
- 12 small mirrors.

This drawing by Sergeant Patrick Gass shows the Corps meeting with Native Americans in the Missouri River Valley.

Winter at Fort Mandan

(December 1804 to March 1805)

The first six months on the river had been hard on the men. They were often wet from pulling the boats in the water. They suffered from snakebites and sunstroke. Stomach ailments were common because of the poor diet. One man died from what was probably a ruptured appendix.

The Corps made plans to spend the winter in camp. Lewis and Clark chose to build a fort in the territory of the Mandan. The Mandan, Native American farmers, hunters, and traders, lived in what is today central North Dakota. Their two villages were set high above the Missouri River.

The site that Lewis and Clark chose for their fort was several miles from the Mandan villages. The captains named it Fort Mandan in

▲ This painting by George Catlin shows a Mandan village.

These photos show a reconstructed Fort Mandan. The fort was made of logs from cottonwood trees. The living quarters had stone fireplaces and chimneys.

honor of the Mandan, who were very friendly and welcomed the Corps.

Lewis and Clark traded with the Mandan for food and sent some of the Corps on a buffalo hunt with the Mandan. They found few buffalo but enough deer and elk to supply them with fresh meat.

The Corps had a portable blacksmith forge. In exchange for food, the men of the Corps who had experience as blacksmiths sharpened hoes, axes, and other tools for the Mandan. The blacksmiths also made new tools for them.

In the Mandan villages that winter, Lewis and Clark met Toussaint Charbonneau (Too-SAN Shar-bon-OH) and his Shoshone wife, Sacajawea. Charbonneau was a French Canadian trader who had lived among Native Americans for some time. As a child, Sacajawea had lived farther west, in the area through which the Corps would be traveling.

▲ Sacajawea accompanied Lewis and Clark on their expedition and served as interpreter and guide. Her contribution is honored on a silver dollar.

IT'S A FACT!

As a young girl, Sacajawea had been captured by the Hidatsa, who kept her prisoner. Charbonneau had bought her as a wife the year before they met Lewis and Clark. She was about 16 years old when she set off with the Corps of Discovery.

In addition to negotiating with the Shoshone, she helped the expedition in other ways. She dug wild plants and picked wild berries to add to their meals. When one of the pirogues began to sink, she saved equipment, medicine, and Indian presents.

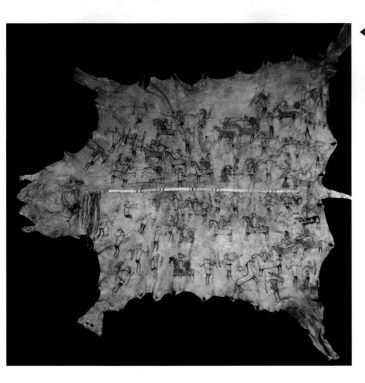

This buffalo robe is one of many things that Lewis and Clark sent back to Jefferson. A Mandan had painted it as a record of a battle with Mandan enemies.

The two captains arranged to take Charbonneau, Sacajawea, and their baby son, Jean-Baptiste, on the expedition. Charbonneau would act as an interpreter and guide. Sacajawea would act as an interpreter and negotiate for horses when the Corps reached the Shoshone.

The Corps had a final job to do before they broke camp. They had to prepare the plant and animal specimens and notes to be sent back to President Jefferson. These items were packed in crates and stored on the keelboat. Seven or eight soldiers set off on the keelboat **downriver** to St. Louis. The others set off upstream to the Pacific.

From Fort Mandan to the Pacific Ocean

(April to December 1805)

As the Corps set off, the Mandan warned them about grizzly bears. The men weren't worried—until they met one! One grizzly bear followed the men into the river. Only a bullet to its head saved the men. For the rest of the trip, the men were in fear of grizzly bears.

The challenge of the Great Falls of the Missouri River awaited the Corps. According to the Mandan, the falls would be easy to get around. Lewis and Clark had expected a single waterfall that would take a half day to **portage**. What they found instead was a series of five waterfalls!

▲ None of the Corps had ever seen a grizzly bear before!

▲ Clark sketched the Great Falls in his journal. This is what the Great Falls look like today.

The first waterfall was 280 yards wide and 97 feet high. That's almost the width of three football fields and the height of a 10-story building. To get their boats and supplies around the falls, the men made their canoes into carts. They cut trees and made wheels from the trunks. They tied the wheels onto the bottoms of the canoes. Then they placed the supplies in the canoes and rolled the canoes on the wheels.

It took the Corps 11 days and five trips to get everything around the falls. Their route up and down hills and around rocks measured about 18 miles.

Earlier on the trip, the Corps had buried one pirogue loaded with food for their return trip. Now they buried the second pirogue full of food. Once they got around the falls, the Corps had to carve more dugout canoes to take the place of the two buried boats.

From the Mandan, Lewis and Clark had learned that the Missouri River would soon end. They would have to cross mountains before they could come to another river. They thought crossing the mountains would take only two or three days. What they didn't realize was that they were facing a series of very wide, very high, and very rugged mountains.

IT'S A FACT!

The Continental Divide is an imaginary line that runs down the spine of the Rocky Mountains. Rivers to the west of this line flow west. Rivers to the east of this line flow east. The Lewis and Clark expedition crossed the Continental Divide on August 12, 1805. They had been traveling for 15 months and had come 3,000 miles.

Lewis and Clark did not know about the Rocky Mountains. In fact, no American knew about the Rockies. The captains also did not realize how far they still were from the Pacific Ocean.

In mid-August, the two men came face to face with the mountains and realized their mistake. The Corps would need horses to get over them.

Lewis and Clark were eager to find the Shoshone, who had horses. As the Corps traveled farther west, Sacajawea began to recognize the land. She told the captains that they were nearing where the Shoshone lived.

The Corps split into two groups. Lewis and one group went ahead looking for Shoshone. They finally found a band. Lewis persuaded the chief, Cameahwait, to go with him to meet Clark and the rest of the Corps.

▲ The Corps, needing horses, went in search of the Shoshone. It is quite likely that the Shosone, from the vantage point of the mountains, saw the Corps before the Corps spotted them.

Sacajawea had stayed with Clark's group. When she saw Cameahwait, she was overcome with joy. The chief was her brother. Sacajawea and the Corps returned to Cameahwait's camp. This was the Shoshone band from which Sacajawea had been captured. The captains bought horses and hired a Shoshone guide for the rugged trail ahead.

The Corps couldn't take their canoes and all their supplies with them over the Rocky Mountains. They buried the supplies they didn't need or couldn't carry on horseback. They sank their canoes in a pond.

With their Shoshone guide, the Corps entered the Bitterroot Mountains. The Bitterroots are part of the Rockies. The Corps followed the Lolo Trail, which runs for 95 miles. It was the most rugged part of the trip.

The Lolo Trail was really just a steep and rocky footpath. There was dense forest all around. The weather

IT'S A FACT!

President Jefferson had instructed Lewis and Clark to look for an all-water route to the Pacific. If they had found such a route, it would have been the Northwest Passage that early European explorers had tried to find. Instead, Lewis and Clark found the Rocky Mountains in the way. There were no rivers that went the whole way through the Rockies. The idea of the Northwest Passage was abandoned.

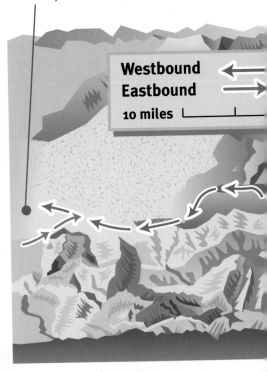

Nez Percé village, Sept. 20, 1805

Westbound ←
Eastbound →
10 miles

was very cold and snowy. The trail was hard to find at times. The men often went on foot and used the horses only to carry the supplies.

Few animals lived in the mountains. The men shot only five deer and a dozen or so birds for food. There were 33 people to feed. One night the men killed one of their horses to eat. Much of the time, the expedition ate the portable soup.

Finally, on September 22, the expedition reached a village of Nez Percé, Native Americans. It had taken the Corps 12 exhausting days to travel the Lolo Trail.

The Lolo Trail

Sept. 9–10, 1805 (trip out)
June 30 to July 2, 1806 (trip back)

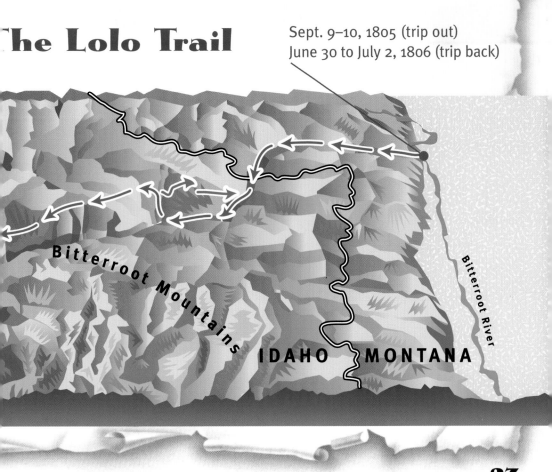

Bitterroot Mountains

Bitterroot River

IDAHO   MONTANA

Lewis and Clark were able to buy food from the Nez Percé for their starving Corps. For a few days, they ate, rested, and made new canoes. They also left some of their horses.

With the help of a Nez Percé guide, the Corps set off on the Clearwater River. Because they had crossed the Continental Divide, the Corps were now going downriver, with the flow of the rivers. On the eastern side of the Continental Divide, the men had been going upstream, against the flow of the Missouri River.

☑ Point

REREAD

Through what rivers did the expedition travel to reach the Pacific Ocean?

▲ This photo of the Nez Percé was probably taken in the 1890s. The Nez Percé had never seen European Americans before the Corps of Discovery came through their land.

▲ "Ocean in view! O! the joy," wrote Clark in his journal. Unfortunately, the Corps had mistaken a wide bay for the Pacific. They still had 20 miles to travel to reach the ocean.

Making 30 miles and more a day, the Corps soon found the Snake River. From there, they floated through the Columbian Plain. They were getting closer to the Columbia River and to the Pacific Ocean.

Excitement was mounting. On October 6, they reached the Columbia River itself. On November 7, they thought they saw the Pacific, but they were only at one end of a wide bay.

High winds, rain, and huge waves kept the Corps from paddling the last few miles to the Pacific. Lewis and Clark decided that the river was too dangerous. Those who wished to see the ocean up close had to walk those last few miles.

The Return Trip

(March to September 1806)

The Corps of Discovery had achieved their goal. They had reached the Pacific Ocean, although they hadn't found an all-water route.

They could not stay out in the open by the river for the winter. Lewis and Clark gave the Corps—including York and Sacajawea—a vote in where they would winter. The Corps voted to go across the Columbia River to its south shore. There, they hoped to find better shelter from the weather. They also hoped to find deer and elk to hunt. The group badly needed food and new clothes. Deer and elk skins would make sturdy shirts and pants.

It took the Corps two weeks to build Fort Clatsop, which they named after a group of Native Americans in the area. On Christmas Day 1805, the Corps settled in to wait out the winter.

▲ Fort Clatsop had a wall around it and a gate. Today the re-created fort is a national memorial.

▲ The enlisted men had three rooms to share. Lewis and Clark had their own rooms. There was also a room for Sacajawea, Charbonneau, and Jean-Baptiste.

Almost three years after they had begun their expedition, Lewis and Clark and the Corps set off on their journey home on March 23, 1806. By early May, they had reached the Nez Percé village again. They picked up the horses they had left there in November.

No Nez Percé was willing to guide the Corps along the Lolo Trail. The Nez Percé said the snow was too deep. The Corps attempted to make the journey without guides, but the snow was 8 to 12 feet deep and the Corps had to turn back. After a delay, two Nez Percé agreed to act as guides. The snow had melted some, and the Corps was able to make it back through the Bitterroot Mountains.

After they got through the Bitterroot Mountains, the Corps split into three groups. One group headed for the Great Falls to dig up the supplies they had left on the trip out. Clark and Lewis each took a group and set off in different directions to explore more of the area. Sacajawea went with Clark's group.

The groups met again at a spot on the Missouri River.

From there they traveled to the Mandan villages. Sacajawea, Charbonneau, and Jean-Baptiste, now a toddler, left the Corps. It was mid-August. In five weeks, the Corps would be back in St. Louis.

✓ Point

READ MORE ABOUT IT

The year 2003 marked the 200th anniversary of the beginning of the Lewis and Clark expedition. Many places along their route held celebrations to honor the men and woman who made this historic journey. For information on some of the most important sites, visit

Fort Mandan:
fortmandan.com

Nez Percé National Historic Park:
nps.gov/nepe

Fort Clatsop:
nps.gov.focl

◀ This monument to Sacajawea is in Portland, Oregon.

A few days from St. Louis, the Corps stopped in several towns along the Missouri River. In each town, the people reacted with astonishment. They thought that the Corps had died on their trip.

On September 23, the Corps members reached St. Louis.

IT'S A FACT!

DISTANCE: 7,600 miles
TIME: 28 months
COST: $2,500
($39,550 in today's dollars)
NEW PLANTS IDENTIFIED: 178
NEW ANIMALS IDENTIFIED: 122

From there, Lewis sent a letter to Jefferson. It said in part:

It is with pleasure that I announce to you the safe arrival of myself and my party at 12 o'clock today. . . In obedience to your orders we have penetrated the Continent of North America to the Pacific Ocean.

With these simple words, Captain Lewis reported the end of one of the most exciting and important journeys across North America. Fur trappers, traders, and farmers would follow the example set by this small band of explorers as they, too, went west.

▼ This statue of Lewis, Clark, and Sacajawea is located in Fort Benton, Montana, facing the Missouri River. It honors all the members of the Lewis and Clark expedition.

The Expedition
1804-1806

② **December 1804 to March 1805**

- Enter Mandan country.
- Build Fort Mandan.
- Hunt buffalo with Mandan.
- Hire Charbonneau and Sacajawea.

① **May to November 1804**

- Pull keelboat off a sandbar.
- First sight of the Great Plains
- Friendly meeting with Missouri and Oto.
- Friendly meeting with Yankton Sioux.
- Unfriendly meeting with Teton Sioux.

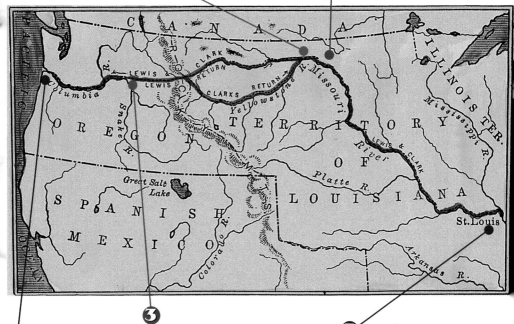

④

January to February 1806

- Build Fort Clatsop.

③

April to December 1805

- Encounter first grizzly bears.
- Portage around the Great Falls.
- Cross the Continental Divide.
- Find Shoshone.
- Buy horses from Shoshone.
- Cross the Bitterroot Mountains on the Lolo Trail.
- Reach a Nez Percé village.
- Travel downriver on the Columbia.
- Reach the Pacific.

⑤

March to September 1806

- Return upstream on the Columbia.
- Return to Nez Percé village.
- Cross the Bitterroot Mountains on the Lolo Trail.
- Return to Mandan village.
- Leave Sacajawea, Charbonneau, and Jean-Baptiste.
- Return to St. Louis.

30

Glossary

band (BAND) group of people (page 12)

compass (KUM-pess) instrument with a magnetic arrow that shows direction (page 12)

downriver (DOWN-rih-vur) direction in which a river flows from its source to its mouth (page 17)

dugout canoe (DUG-owt KUH-noo) boat made by digging out the center of a log (page 9)

expedition (EX-puh-dih-shun) a journey undertaken for a specific purpose (page 4)

Great Plains (GRAY-t PLAY-nz) huge area of flatland and grasses stretching across the center of the United States from north to south and east to west (page 11)

journal (JUR-nuhl) diary or record that a person writes (page 5)

keelboat (KEEL-boht) shallow boat used on the Mississippi and Missouri rivers to carry freight (page 8)

knapsack (NAP-sak) leather or canvas bag worn across a person's back; like a backpack (page 7)

Northwest Passage (NORTH-west PAS-ej) the all-water route through North America thought to exist but proven not to (page 4)

pirogue (PEH-rohg) a boat shaped like a canoe but larger (page 9)

pole (POHL) to push a boat along with a pole (page 8)

portage (POR-taj) carrying a boat around waterfalls or from river to river (page 18)

sandbar (SAND-bar) area of rising sand in the bottom of a river (page 10)

specimen (SPES-ih-men) an example (page 5)

upstream (UP-streem) direction in which a river flows from its mouth to its source (page 9)

Index

band, 12, 21

Bitterroot Mountains, 22, 27–28

Cameahwait, 21

Charbonneau, Toussaint, 16–17, 28

Clark, William, 4–6, 8, 10, 12, 14–18, 20–22, 24–28

Clearwater River, 24

Columbian Plain, 25

Columbia River, 25

compass, 12

Continental Divide, 20, 24

Corps of Discovery, 5-29

downriver, 17

dugout canoe, 9, 19

Fort Clatsop, 26

Fort Mandan, 14–15

Great Falls, 18–19, 28

Great Plains, 11

Jefferson Peace Medal, 12

Jefferson, Thomas, 1–6, 12, 17, 22, 29

journal, 5, 10

keelboat, 8-10, 17

knapsack, 7

Lewis, William, 4–8, 10, 12–18, 20-22, 24–29

Lolo Trail, 22–23

Louisiana Territory, 2–4

Madison, James, 3

Mandan, 14–16, 18, 20, 28

Mississippi River, 2, 10

Missouri River, 10-12, 14, 18, 20, 28

New Orleans, 2

Nez Percé, 23–24, 27

Northwest Passage, 4, 22

pirogue, 9, 16, 19

pole, 8, 9

Rocky Mountains, 20–22

Sacajawea, 16–17, 21, 26, 28

sandbar, 10

Seaman, 10

Shoshone, 16–17, 21-22

Snake River, 25

specimen, 5, 17

St. Louis, 7, 10, 28, 29

Teton Sioux, also known as Lakota, 13

upstream, 9, 10

Yankton Sioux, 12

York, 7, 26